EXCAVATING THE PAST

# ANCIENT ROME

*Fiona Macdonald*

Heinemann Library
Chicago, Illinois

© 2005 Heinemann Library
a division of Reed Elsevier Inc.
Chicago, Illinois

Customer Service 888-454-2279
Visit our website at www.heinemannlibrary.com

Designed by Tamarillo Design
Originated by Ambassador Litho Ltd
Printed in China by WKT Company Limited


09 08 07 06 05
10 9 8 7 6 5 4 3 2 1

**Library of Congress Cataloging-in-Publication Data**
Macdonald, Fiona.
  Ancient Rome / Fiona Macdonald.
    p. cm. -- (Excavating the past)
Includes bibliographical references and index.
  ISBN 1-4034-4838-8 (Library Binding-hardcover) -- ISBN 1-4034-5458-2 (Paperback)
  1. Rome--Civilization--Juvenile literature. 2. Rome--Antiquities--Juvenile literature. [1. Rome--Civilization. 2. Rome--Antiquities.] I. Title. II. Series.
  DG77.M248 2004
  937--dc22

                            2003023730

**Acknowledgments**
The author and publisher are grateful to the following for permission to reproduce photographs: pp. 5 top and bottom, 6, 9, 10, 11, 14, 15 top and bottom, 18 top, 20, 22, 23 bottom, 26, 31 top and bottom, 32, 33 top and bottom, 34 bottom, 39 top and center, 41 top Art Archive; pp. 7 Bridgeman Art Libary; pp. 8, 12, 40 top and bottom, 41 bottom left and right British Museum; pp. 13 top, 28 top, 29, 34 top, 35 top, 27 top and bottom, 42 all Corbis; p. 16 Cassandra Vivian; p. 17 top Skyscan; pp. 18 bottom, 19 top and bottom, 21 top and bottom, 30, 43 Alamy; pp. 23 top, 28 bottom, 36 center and bottom, 38 all Scala Picture Library; pp. 24–25 all, 27 top Fishbourne Roman Palace; pp. 27 bottom CM Dixon.

Cover photograph of the Colosseum reproduced with permission of Alamy. The small photograph of the legionnaire's helmet reproduced with permission of Corbis.

Every effort has been made to contact copyright holders of any material reproduced in this book. Any omissions will be rectified in subsequent printings if notice is given to the publisher.

Some words are shown in bold, **like this.** You can find out what they mean by looking in the glossary.

# CONTENTS

# THE ROMAN WORLD

From around 300 B.C.E. to C.E. 300, the ancient Romans were the most powerful people in the world. They ruled a vast **empire** from Rome, their magnificent capital city. Their army was very strong, their government was well-organized, and their laws were respected and punishments feared. Taxes and trade made them rich. They liked good food, cruel sports, and big houses. They were also expert builders and **engineers**.

▽ *Around C.E. 117, the Roman empire was at its greatest. It included large parts of Europe, north Africa, and the Middle East. The names in parentheses are the earlier names.*

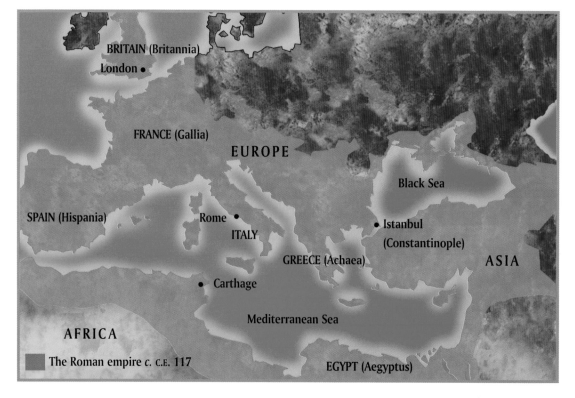

BRITAIN (Britannia)
London •
FRANCE (Gallia)
EUROPE
Black Sea
SPAIN (Hispania)
Rome •
ITALY
• Istanbul
(Constantinople)
GREECE (Achaea)
ASIA
• Carthage
Mediterranean Sea
AFRICA
The Roman empire c. C.E. 117
EGYPT (Aegyptus)

## The end of an empire

The Roman empire collapsed around 1,550 years ago. It was weakened by fights among its rulers, and attacks from warlike tribes from Central Asia. Roman cities, towns, and **forts** were abandoned or destroyed. Toward the end, in C.E. 395, the Roman empire was divided into two halves, east and west, but later it split into many smaller states.

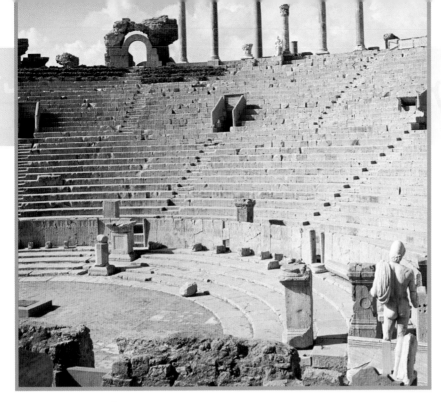

◁ *These are the **ruins** of a theater from the 1st century C.E. at Leptis Magna, Libya, in north Africa. By studying the remains of Roman buildings, archaeologists have learned about Roman building skills. They also ask: Who designed this building? What was its purpose? Who used it? Why was it planned this way?*

## Roman remains

For a while, the Roman civilization was forgotten—but it did not completely disappear. We still drive along Roman roads, and many European languages include Roman words. We give children Roman names, such as "Antony" or "Julia." Books and films about the Romans are very popular, and in big cities we can see important buildings, such as banks, museums, and even churches, built in the Roman style.

Most important of all, we remember the Romans today because we can see the evidence they left behind. Remains of Roman homes, **temples**, markets, and **bathhouses** survive in many lands the Romans once ruled, together with all kinds of **artifacts**— from beautiful jewelry to worn-out shoes.

▷ *A Roman family from the 3rd century C.E. is carved on an elaborate coffin from the Valley of Tombs in Syria. How did they spend their free time? Archaeology can help us find out about their lives.*

DID YOU KNOW? The city of Rome was built on seven hills with a defensive stone wall around it. **5**

## How Roman archaeology developed

Around C.E. 1200, visitors to Rome from Europe were shocked to see grass growing in the streets and cows grazing among the remains of ancient buildings. The ordinary people of Rome were too poor to care for their ancient city. And the richest, most powerful people—leaders of the Christian Church—did not value the non-Christian, Roman remains.

### Re-birth of the ancient Romans

During the 1300s, attitudes changed. Writers, **scholars**, architects, and artists began to base their work on the study of the world around them— and on the investigation of ancient remains. This movement became known as the Renaissance (re-birth). Renaissance artists copied ancient Roman statues, and architects used many features from ancient Roman buildings in their designs. They made drawings of Roman **ruins** and of newly discovered works of art, and published descriptions of them in books, thanks to the latest technology—printing. They saw ancient Rome in a new way—as a civilization with values and achievements to copy and admire. In spite of this interest, the first organized **excavations** of Roman sites were not made until the 1700s. Since then, archaeologists studying ancient Rome have developed many new techniques to make sense of the evidence the Romans left behind.

### Rediscovered

This marble statue, carved in Rome around C.E. 100, shows a scene from a Roman **legend.** After Roman power collapsed, the statue disappeared. It was rediscovered in the 1400s and put on display in Rome in the Pope's famous sculpture collection. There, it caused a sensation and was greatly admired.

## Grand Tour

From the late 1600s to the early 1800s, young men from wealthy European families were sent on the "Grand Tour" to complete their education. They visited historic sites in Italy, and sometimes Greece, to admire the remains of ancient civilizations. Their visits encouraged Roman archaeology in two ways. They always wanted to see new excavations and admire new "treasures." They also wanted to buy examples of Roman art to take home as souvenirs.

▽ *This 18th century painting by John Feary is titled, "Rome Seen on a Grand Tour."*

## Making use of the past

Many politicians have studied Roman history and archaeology. Some hope it will teach them useful lessons about government. But others aim to steal some of ancient Rome's glory for themselves. In the 1930s, Italian **dictator** Benito Mussolini gave orders for public buildings to be designed in classical Roman style, but he destroyed many ancient ruins to do so.

## WHO WAS Johann Joachim Winckelmann?

Winckelmann was born in Germany in 1717. He studied the art and architecture of ancient Greece and Rome. In 1763, he went to Rome to work as the Pope's "antiquary" (historian and archaeologist). Before his death in 1768, Winckelmann published books that inspired many other scholars to continue studying after him. He wrote, "the only way to become great . . . is by copying the ancients."

DID YOU KNOW? Before 1700, poor people used bricks from ancient Roman buildings to build their own homes. **7**

# ROMAN VOICES

**W**ritten evidence is one of the most important sources of information about past times because it allows ancient people to "speak" to us and tell us about themselves and how they lived. A great deal of writing survives from ancient Rome.

## Discoveries at Vindolanda

Some of the most interesting writing from Roman times comes from private letters, sent by ordinary people to their families and friends. In 1973, an amazing collection of documents was found at Vindolanda, a ruined Roman **fort** near Hadrian's Wall, in northern Great Britain.

Reading the Vindolanda letters is like hearing voices from the past. Soldiers ask for little luxuries to make their lives more comfortable—and reveal that they are suffering badly from the cold British climate. Almost in reply, one writer says he has sent wool socks and two pairs of underpants to the fort. The letters uncover everyday army life. Some letters describe enemy soldiers—whom the commander calls *Brittunculi* ("wretched little Brits").

△ *More than a thousand letters, lists, and reports written to, or by, the commander of the fort, his family, the fort's officers, and ordinary soldiers, have been found so far. The tablets provide the best picture of life in the Roman army anywhere in the world.*

# WHO IS Robin Birley?

*Robin Birley, who discovered the Vindolanda letters, belongs to a family with a special interest in the Vindolanda Roman fort. Robin has worked at Vindolanda for more than 50 years. His father, Professor Eric Birley, owned the Vindolanda site, and began the first* **excavations** *there from 1930 to 1936. His house has been turned into the Vindolanda Museum. Robin's brother, Anthony, is a professor with a special interest in Roman history, and his son, Andrew, is also an archaeologist at Vindolanda.*

## Vindolanda letters

The Vindolanda letters date from between C.E. 90 and 120. They were written in Latin, the Romans' language, on thin leaves of wood about the size of a modern postcard. Writers used a metal pen, and ink made from soot. As well as giving an idea of life at the **fort**, the Vindolanda letters also provide valuable evidence of language, spelling, grammar, and handwriting styles. They record information about local place names in northern England, and the prices paid for food and drink.

## Archaeology Challenge

The Vindolanda letters are very fragile. When exposed to the air, the wood breaks up and the writing fades away. The challenge facing archaeologists is to stop them from decaying, so that people can see and read them in the future. After careful experiments, **conservators** working on the Vindolanda letters found that soaking them in a special mixture of alcohol, then allowing them to dry, stopped the crumbling or fading. They also cleaned the letters by picking up tiny specks of dirt with the point of a needle, using a microscope to avoid scratching the surface of the letters.

◁ *This wall painting from Pompeii shows a couple who could read and write. The man is holding a scroll of papyrus (paper made from reeds), which was used for important documents. The woman is holding a wax-covered writing tablet, used for making notes, and a stylus (pointed stick) to write with.*

DID YOU KNOW? The Vindolanda letters were put on a Roman bonfire, but it rained so the letters survived.

## Scholars, poets, and civil servants

As well as letters, many other kinds of written evidence survive from Roman times. Government leaders and **scholars** wrote down their ideas about politics, **philosophy**, and the law. Historians, like Tacitus, recorded the rise of Roman power, and helped Roman **citizens** learn about their past. Army commanders, like Julius Caesar, wrote detailed descriptions of their great battles and successful **campaigns**, and wrote about themselves as heroes.

## Writing for entertainment

Reading and writing could also be fun. Roman men, and quite a few women, enjoyed poems, plays, and dramatic stories. The Roman author Petronius wrote the world's first novel about a group of travelers in Italy. Many citizens visited libraries and book stores in search of the latest publications. Favorite authors included Ovid, who wrote love poems and fantasy tales based on ancient legends, and Terence, a freed slave from Africa who wrote comic plays. Works by Roman travelers, describing foreign lands and the strange, "**barbarian**" peoples who lived there, were also popular. The descriptions made Roman people feel sure that their own civilization was the best.

## Behind the scenes

This Roman **mosaic** from the 1st century C.E. shows actors and musicians rehearsing before a performance. At first, plays were part of religious festivals. Later they were put on just for entertainment. Many plots were copied from earlier Greek dramas. Plays were paid for by rich Romans, who gave out free tickets to gain popularity. All the actors were men. They wore masks when acting female roles, and sang and danced, as well as spoke their lines.

## Slogans, graffiti, and curses

Supporters of rival politicians scribbled **slogans** on walls and doors. Ordinary men and women added graffiti, sending romantic messages to their boyfriends and girlfriends, praising **gladiators** and other local heroes, or criticizing proud, rich citizens. Writing was also used to make public displays of government **propaganda.** There were carved inscriptions on Roman monuments and public buildings to honor the Roman state or record Roman triumphs in war.

▽ *This poster from Pompeii features news of an election, 1st century C.E.*

### EYEWITNESS

"Claudia Severa sends greetings to her friend Lepidina. Sister, please come to visit us on the third day before the Ides of September, to celebrate my birthday . . . It will make the day much more enjoyable for me."

*Letter from the wife of the fort commander at Vindolanda to one of her female friends*

## Writing for administration

To help the government run smoothly, Roman leaders kept many written records, such as lists of elected officials or money paid as taxes. **Civil servants** stored this information on neat scrolls, kept in government archives. Coins carried the names of ruling emperors, and tombs of famous men were inscribed with their official titles.

## Fantasy or Fact?

*Throughout their empire, the Romans spoke a language called Latin. Today, people often call Latin a "dead language." But is this true? We still use many Latin words today, 2,000 years after the Romans ruled.*
*Here are some examples:*
*animal, antique, chorus, circus, color, fungus, horror, labor, sinister, spectator, superior, victor, virus.*

At first, Rome was ruled by kings. Then, in 509 B.C.E., it became a **republic**. This meant that Roman **citizens** could vote for elected officials, who took advice from **senators**. In 27 B.C.E., an army commander was elected **emperor** and took the title "Augustus" (honored). Emperors ruled after him until Roman power collapsed in C.E. 476.

The city of Rome, in central Italy, lay at the heart of the Roman **empire**. It was the center of Roman government, law, learning, and religion. It was also a big, busy, and crowded trading town, home to families from all over Italy and from other lands ruled by Rome. From around 30 B.C.E. to C.E. 400, it was the largest city in the world. The area was a natural site for settlement. It was on a river and close to the sea, but far enough inland to be safe from pirates. The surrounding hills also gave protection from attacks.

▽ *Below are ruined buildings in the Forum at Rome, drawn by Piranesi in 1757, before Rodolfo Lanciani began his work to save them. The area looks quiet and deserted. This was very different from Roman times, when the Forum would be full of people listening to politicians' rousing speeches.*

## WHO WAS Rodolfo Lanciani?

*Born in Italy in 1847, Lanciani was one of the first archaeologists to study the ancient Roman civilization in an organized way. He made a set of 46 maps of ancient Rome that are still very highly regarded. When he lived, Rome was growing fast, and many ancient sites were threatened by new roads, buildings, and underground **engineering** works. As Director of **Excavations** in Rome, he recorded vital evidence that would otherwise have been lost forever.*

◁ *This archway was built by Emperor Septimus Severus in C.E. 203, to commemorate the tenth anniversary of his reign. It is decorated with carvings showing scenes from his wars against Parthia (now Iran and Iraq) and Arabia.*

## The Forum and other Roman districts

Rome was built on seven hills, separated by steep valleys. There was no overall building plan and even citizens got lost among its maze of narrow, twisting streets, shopping malls, and public squares. At the center was the Forum, an open space surrounded by beautiful buildings. Originally it was a marketplace, but it soon became the religious and business center of the city.

The Forum was rebuilt several times, with **temples**, law courts, and business centers. After around C.E. 470, these were all abandoned, and slowly crumbled and collapsed. By around 1800, they were almost all in **ruins**. They were saved from total destruction by pioneer architects, like Rodolfo Lanciani, who stopped the ruins from being torn down to make room for new buildings.

Elsewhere there were magnificent sports arenas, public libraries, and **bathhouses**, as well as fine homes for the rich and cramped lodgings for the poor. Each district had its own character. The most exclusive area was the Palatine Hill. This was where Rome's governing classes had their homes.

### Archaeology Challenge

Also known as "salvage archaeology," rescue archaeology is designed to gather as much information as possible from a site before it is destroyed, or buried under new buildings. Rescue archaeologists work fast in teams to **survey** the site, record all that they find there, and **conserve** moveable objects, samples of soil, photographs, drawings, and other evidence for future study.

## Big city life

Wealthy Romans had comfortable town houses, surrounded by strong walls for safety and privacy, and cool courtyard gardens. The rooms had high ceilings, wide doors, and brightly painted walls. The floors were often covered with **mosaics**—tiny cubes of colored pottery, stone, or glass, arranged to make pictures or patterns. There was not much furniture. Wooden chairs and couches, used for sleeping and for reclining on one side to eat meals, were decorated with paintings and carvings. Dim, flickering light was provided by pottery lamps that burned olive oil.

Poor Romans lived in crowded apartment blocks, three or four stories high. Each block was divided into many small rooms. The biggest and best were on the first floor and had balconies. The dirtiest and noisiest, often used as stores, were at street level. The smallest rooms were under the roof.

◁ *This is a 1st century C.E. floor mosaic from Pompeii. Some Romans had guard dogs to keep their property safe. A mosaic has been found with the message "cave canem," which means "beware of the dog."*

## High-rise homes

This reconstructed model in the Museo della Civilta, Rome, is based on the excavated remains of an apartment block in Ostia, the port of Rome. The Romans called these blocks *insulae*, or islands, because each one was a separate community. Apartment blocks were baking hot in summer, and very cold in winter. The upper rooms were damp because the cheap tiled roofs leaked when it rained. Many blocks were destroyed by fire, because families cooked over open fires in their rooms.

## Going shopping

Slaves from rich families, and housewives from poor ones, went shopping every day to buy food. Rome also had shops selling books, perfumes, medicines, clothes, tools, household goods, and luxury items imported from distant lands. These luxury items included silk from China, spices from India, hunting dogs from Great Britain, and blond hair from Germany, which was used to make wigs.

△ *These public toilets in Leptis Magna, Libya, date from the 2nd century* C.E.

## Water, toilets, and drains

This aqueduct was built around C.E. 100 in Nîmes, France. Romans were expert **engineers.** They built aqueducts, which were like high bridges, to carry water to cities and towns. Water flowed inside a channel at the top. The channel ended in a **reservoir** from which water was piped to rich people's homes, and to public fountains, where poor people could collect it. The Romans also built public toilets on street corners and a huge sewer, called the *Cloaca Maxima* (1,969 feet; 600 meters long), beneath Rome, to carry waste to the Tiber River.

DID YOU KNOW? The *Cloaca Maxima* (main sewer) was so big that you could row along it in a boat. **15**

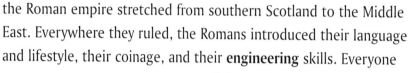

# ARMY AND EMPIRE

R oman power grew quickly. By around 300 B.C.E., the Romans controlled all Italy and, from there, advanced to conquer a vast **empire**. At its greatest, in around C.E. 117, the Roman empire stretched from southern Scotland to the Middle East. Everywhere they ruled, the Romans introduced their language and lifestyle, their coinage, and their **engineering** skills. Everyone living in the empire had to pay Roman taxes and obey Roman laws.

▷ *This mudbrick Roman fortress with its distinctive square towers is in Ain Umm Dabadib, in Egypt's western desert.*

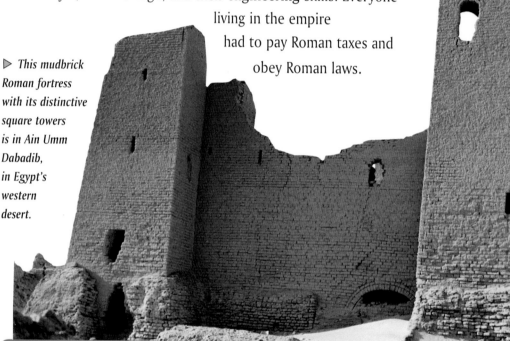

## WHO WAS John Clayton?

*John Clayton (1792–1890) was a lawyer. His family owned a large house with Roman remains in the fields nearby. His father covered the ruins to create a park, but John dug them up again, discovering Chesters Fort. He bought large sections of Hadrian's Wall to stop local farmers from taking its stones away, excavated a Roman army **temple,** and opened a museum to display his finds. John Clayton was untrained and did his excavating in an unscientific way, but his achievements were remarkable, especially because he was so busy—he only did archaeology on Mondays!*

▷ *This aerial photograph shows the outline of Housesteads Fort in northern England. Forts like this would have been home to a **legion**, that is about 5,000 Roman soldiers and commanders.*

## Network of roads

The city of Rome was linked to other cities, **forts**, and army camps by a network of well-made roads. Roads were often built by the army so that soldiers could move quickly into battle, and messengers carry urgent instructions to officials in distant empire lands. As the Romans themselves boasted, "all roads led to Rome."

## Hadrian's Wall and its forts

Roman armies conquered this great empire, and they kept it under control. They were stationed in camps and forts— permanent army bases, made of wood and stone. They also built huge defenses like Hadrian's Wall in northern England, which ran for 75 miles (120 kilometers). Some of the largest Roman forts, such as Housesteads, were built nearby, to guard the northern frontier of the empire, and stop enemy peoples invading. Roman soldiers left Great Britain soon after C.E. 400. Their camps and forts all along Hadrian's Wall were looted for building materials, and became overgrown. Since the 1800s, archaeologists have followed the example set by John Clayton at Housesteads, excavating the remains of the forts to find out how they were planned and built, and how soldiers lived there.

## Archaeology Challenge

Today, archaeologists use several techniques to investigate what lies beneath the surface of the ground. Resistivity uses an electric current to detect hidden differences under the soil. Magnetometry shows if natural patterns of magnetism in the ground have been disturbed by human activity. Both can give archaeologists clues to help them find buried buildings, ditches, or graves. **Aerial** photography reveals the outlines of underground objects, showing up as differences of height or color among growing crops.

DID YOU KNOW? Hadrian's Wall took seven years to build, and used 27,192,293 cubic feet of stone. **17**

## Roman soldiers

The Roman army was a well-trained, professional fighting force. It contained about 150,000 **legionaries** (foot soldiers, who were Roman **citizens**), plus many **auxiliary** ("helper") soldiers from Roman empire lands. They all signed up to serve for between 20 and 25 years. If they survived, they were given land and a **pension** when they retired. The army was divided into **legions** of about 5,000 men, and smaller **centuries** of about 80 soldiers, each commanded by a **centurion**. It was his duty to keep order, and lead his men into battle.

△ *This carving from the 2nd century C.E. shows officers and soldiers from the Praetorian Guard. This was a special unit of men who served as the emperor's personal bodyguard.*

### A story in stone

Trajan's column is a tall stone pillar, 98 feet (30 meters) high, in the center of Rome. It **commemorates** the **Emperor** Trajan, who ruled the Roman empire from C.E. 98–117. The column is covered from top to bottom with detailed carvings that show Trajan leading his armies to victory in Dacia (now Romania). The carvings provide historians and archaeologists with valuable evidence of Roman weapons, armor, forts, buildings, and fighting techniques.

## Battle tactics

Roman commanders planned their battles carefully, choosing a site that would make fighting difficult for their enemies, and waiting for the right weather, such as dazzling early morning sun. To attack, Roman soldiers advanced in lines, holding their shields in front of them, then hurled their javelins. After this, they charged forward, slashing and stabbing with their swords. A soldier who hesitated or ran away in battle was beaten to death.

## Archaeology Challenge

People interested in the Roman army sometimes try to find out more by taking part in "living history" events. They research the clothes and armor that the soldiers may have worn, and the weapons they may have carried. Then they recreate them, using traditional materials and techniques where possible. They build forts, camps, and war-machines, such as ballistas (giant crossbows), which the Romans used in sieges. They study eyewitness descriptions of old battles, then act them out—taking care that no one gets hurt.

### EYEWITNESS

"They [Roman soldiers] do not wait for war to begin for getting to grips with their weapons, nor are they idle in peacetime . . . they never stop training . . ."

Jewish historian Josephus, C.E. 64

## Weapons and armor

Legionary soldiers were armed with a *pugio* (dagger), *pilum* (javelin), and *gladius* (short iron sword). They wore metal helmets with neck guards and cheek-flaps, body armor made from overlapping strips of iron and tough leather sandals (*caligae*) with metal-studded soles. Auxiliary soldiers fought on horseback, or used their own local weapons, such as bows and arrows or slingshots. Many wore chainmail armor and pants, rather than Roman-style tunics.

▽ *This is a 1st century C.E. iron dagger and sheath from the Roman fort site at Hod Hill, in southern England.*

# WHO DID THE ROMANS WORSHIP?

Romans worshipped a family of gods, headed by Jupiter, "Best and Greatest." He was lord of the sky and special protector of the Roman state. Other honored gods included Mars, god of war; Venus, goddess of love; Minerva, goddess of wisdom; and Juno, who protected women.

## The Pantheon

Romans pictured their gods as looking like humans, but bigger, stronger, and more beautiful. They built a separate **temple** for each of them as a home. They also constructed a magnificent temple, called the Pantheon, to honor all the gods. The Pantheon (built between C.E. 118 and 125) is one of the few Roman buildings to have survived undamaged. This is because around C.E. 609, it was converted into a Christian church. Its new owners removed the statues of Roman gods, but left the rest of the building alone. The tall stone columns, **mosaic** floor, and magnificent domed roof survive almost as they were in Roman times.

▲ *Emperor Marcus Aurelius (C.E. 121–180) makes a sacrifice at a religious ceremony. The Romans feared the gods, and gave them gifts in the hope of getting their help and protection.*

## WHO WAS Marcus Agrippa?

*Marcus Agrippa was chief advisor to Augustus, the first Roman emperor (ruled 27 B.C.E.–C.E. 14). He organized political campaigns to win support for Augustus' new government. To help Augustus gain popularity, he planned massive schemes to rebuild the center of Rome. To win popularity for himself, Marcus built the first Pantheon temple to ask the gods to protect Rome, and huge public baths where Roman **citizens** could relax and keep clean. We can still see his name carved on the front of the Pantheon.*

"When I came to power in Rome, it was a city of brick. I have made it a city of marble."

*Emperor Augustus, around C.E. 12*

▽ *Below is the outside of the Pantheon today. This building is on the site of an earlier temple paid for by the Roman politician Marcus Agrippa.*

Romans believed the gods would help those who pleased them, and punish anyone who offended them. So they gave the gods sacrifices (gifts) of fruit, flowers, and specially killed animals. To remind people that the gods were watching them, public religious celebrations were held throughout the year. These were led by priests and priestesses chosen from the most important families in Rome. Many powerful politicians, including emperors, also served as priests as part of their public duties.

△ *Inside the dome of the Pantheon.*

## Archaeology Challenge

Why was the Pantheon built? To answer questions like this, archaeologists use written evidence—that is, old documents such as **chronicles,** letters, wills, financial accounts, and law-court records, as well as **inscriptions** on buildings. These can reveal important information about the people involved, like Marcus Agrippa, what they thought and believed, and what they hoped to achieve.

# Foreign gods and family gods

From around the 1st century B.C.E., Roman people began to follow new, foreign religions, imported from lands in the Roman **empire**. These included the worship of Isis, Egyptian goddess of new life; Cybele, a mother-goddess from Turkey; and Mithras, a god of light from Persia (now Iran). Many of the gods in the Roman world came from Greek mythology. The Romans gave them new names and personalities. Whereas the Greek gods had a human familiarity, the Roman gods were more powerful and terrifying.

From the 1st century C.E., some Romans became Christians, although they were **persecuted** until C.E. 313. Archaeologists have found Roman-style statues and wall-paintings of these new gods in many parts of the Roman empire, and **temples** built in their honor.

All these new faiths were most unlike traditional Roman religion. Their worshippers took part in mysterious services that were often held in secret. They prayed for new life after death, instead of asking the gods for wealth and power for the Roman state.

## Mystery religion

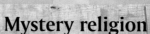

This statue from the 2nd century C.E. shows the god Mithras sacrificing a great bull. Mithras **symbolized** goodness, and many myths told how he fought against evil and brought new life to the world. He was worshipped in dramatic, night-time ceremonies—women were not allowed to take part. He was especially honored by Roman soldiers. They believed he would give them new life after they had been killed in battle.

## Mixed gods

Throughout the empire, Roman and local gods sometimes became mixed together. Sometimes, as in this 2nd century C.E. statue of Anubis, an Egyptian god, a local god is portrayed in Roman style. Elsewhere, Roman conquerors assumed that local gods and goddesses must be the same as their own.

## Family gods

At home, each Roman family worshipped its own private gods: the *Lares* (who guarded the household and family) and *Penates* (who protected the store-cupboard—that is, the family's wealth and well-being). Roman men also honored the "genius" of their family—the **ancestral** spirit that lived in them, and would be passed on to their children when they died.

## Family prayers

At left is a fresco, or wall painting, showing an **altar** of the *Lares* (household gods). Each day, the male head of the family said prayers and made offerings at the family shrine to the *Lares* and *Penates*. The shrine might be a collection of little statues, or an image of the guardian gods painted on the wall. Women prepared food offerings for the gods, and decorated the shrine with flowers on festival days.

# COUNTRY LIFE

**M**ost people in the Roman **empire** lived in the countryside. Farming methods and land ownership varied from country to country, depending on local customs and laws. In Italy, the Romans' homeland, the land was divided into huge **estates** owned by a few rich families. They built large country houses there, called villas, with beautiful gardens and farm buildings nearby. Rich families lived mostly in towns, but visited their villas in the summer to escape the heat. Wherever the Romans conquered, they built country villas for themselves, and encouraged rich local people to do the same.

▽ *Archaeologists have used the evidence from excavations at Fishbourne to create this reconstruction of the villa as it may have looked around C.E. 80.*

## Discovering Fishbourne

In 1960, workers digging a trench for a waterpipe at Fishbourne, in southern England, accidentally disturbed the remains of a Roman building. The site was to be used for housing, but the landowner agreed to let archaeologists investigate. They discovered the largest Roman villa found in Great Britain so far. It had been built in three stages, between around C.E. 43 and 80. The first stage was a small wooden **fort**. The second was a larger stone home. The villa's final stage was so splendid that archaeologists called it a palace.

## WHO WERE the Volunteers?

*In the mid-1900s in Great Britain, when the Fishbourne Roman villa was discovered, most archaeological **excavation** was done by volunteers. They received no pay, but worked because they were interested in the past and felt excited by the idea of taking part in an excavation. Usually, they were directed by paid university professors. At Fishbourne, about 900 volunteers worked for 10 years to uncover the Roman remains.*

◁ *The photograph on the left shows the 1960s excavation of the original Roman bedding trenches in the gardens at Fishbourne. On the right, the garden has been replanted with a box hedge as it was in Roman times.*

## Archaeology Challenge

Pollen analysis, also called **palynology,** is used to study ancient climates and vegetation. With the help of a microscope, archaeologists examine tiny grains of pollen, which can remain in the soil for thousands of years. From these, they hope to identify the plants that once grew on a site such as the Roman gardens at Fishbourne. This tells them whether land was cultivated or left wild, which crops were grown, and when new plants were introduced from foreign lands.

▽ *In the 2nd and 3rd centuries C.E., improvements were added at Fishbourne such as this mosaic floor and a central heating system. Around C.E. 300, when more improvements were about to be made, the villa caught fire. It was gutted, and never lived in again.*

From the evidence of a Roman **inscription** found close by, archaeologists think that the Fishbourne villa may have been built for a British king named Togidubnus, who lived around C.E. 75. He was friendly and peaceable toward the Roman conquerors of Great Britain. In return, they let him rule his kingdom independently. His palace covered more than 226,000 square feet (21,000 square meters).

## Farms and slaves

All the work in villas and estates was done by slaves. In the villa they cooked, cleaned, did the laundry, cared for the owner and his family, ran messages, weeded the garden, and sometimes read, sang, or played music to entertain the villa owner and his guests. On a villa farm, slaves tended crops and gathered the harvest, picked olives and grapes to make oil and wine, milked cows and goats, cared for cart-horses and oxen, sheared sheep, and spun and wove their wool into cloth for everyone on the estate to wear.

### Villa life

This **mosaic** shows a Roman villa in Tunisia, north Africa. In it, you can see slaves hard at work gardening, looking after flocks and herds, hunting, picking olives from a tree, and catching birds to eat. At the bottom of the picture, you can see the owner of the villa (right) and his wife (left), relaxing. She is trying on a necklace; he is receiving a rolled up letter from a messenger.

### Jobs for life

Slaves were not free to leave villas or **estates,** and had very few rights. In law, they could be bought and sold, punished, or even killed by their owners. But they were also valuable property. So, although some slaves were badly treated, others were well looked after and given important jobs, such as running estates and managing farms. Many trusted slaves were set free when their owners died. Others saved up to buy their freedom.

## Plowman at work

This 2nd century C.E. bronze statue shows a farm worker from Roman Britain. He is guiding a heavy plow pulled by a pair of oxen. His task is to uproot any weeds, break down clods of soil, and cut a neat furrow in the ground so that seeds of wheat, oats, or barley can be planted. When they have grown and ripened, they will be reaped (cut) with curved sickles, carted to barns, threshed (hit with sticks) to separate the grains from the ear, then ground by hand between stones to make flour, or stewed for hours over an open fire to make porridge.

### Fantasy or Fact?

*This is how the Roman poet Virgil (70–19 B.C.E.) described life in the countryside:*

*"How fortunate farmers are, if only they knew it! Far away from war, the honest Earth brings them an easy living from the soil ..."*

*Do you think slaves working on large estates would have agreed with him?*

## Slave child

The children of slaves became slaves like their parents. They had to work as soon as they were old enough to be useful. This mosaic shows a young slave boy carrying fruit. Slave boys were sent to climb trees at harvesttime to shake down olives and apples to older slaves waiting below.

# TIME-CAPSULE TOWNS

In C.E. 79, two rich, fashionable seaside towns, Pompeii and Herculaneum, were destroyed when a nearby volcano, Vesuvius, erupted. Some **citizens** escaped by heading out to sea in boats, but many were killed by clouds of poisonous gas released by the volcano. Within 24 hours, the two towns were buried feet deep under ash and lava that preserved almost everything there, as if in a time capsule. The towns remained hidden for almost 1,700 years.

△ You can still see the remains of houses on the Street of Abundance in Pompeii.

## Discovering Pompeii and Herculaneum

In 1710, the Prince of Elbouf, who lived in southern Italy, decided to explore some tunnels made by miners. They were digging into the layers of **pumice** (solid lava) and ash produced by the eruption of Vesuvius, to find pieces of fine marble stone, which local people wanted for their houses. When the prince looked at the marble, he realized that it was Roman remains. He ordered further investigations and it soon became clear that the marble came from Herculaneum. In 1748, the diggers discovered the famous site of Pompeii.

▽ Archaeologists use evidence from excavations to create computer reconstructions of houses in Pompeii. These allow people to explore past buildings from all angles, and even to "walk" though the rooms as they would have looked in Roman times.

The King and Queen of Naples gave money to pay for more **excavations**. They wanted statues and other Roman treasures to add to their royal collections, and so workers simply dug wherever they chose, looking for buried treasures. There was no planned excavation, and so much of the the site where objects lay hidden was destroyed. After 1782, when German **scholar** Johann Joachim Winckelmann published a description of Herculaneum, the "time-capsule" towns attracted visitors from all over Europe and inspired fashions in art, furniture, and interior design. But there was no scientific excavation of the sites until Giuseppe Fiorelli arrived in 1860.

## Archaeology Challenge

Many people in Pompeii were choked to death by poison gas from Vesuvius and were buried under ash and lava, which eventually cooled and solidified. Over the centuries, their bodies decayed, leaving hollow spaces. Normal excavation techniques would have destroyed these hollow spaces. So in 1864, Giuseppe Fiorelli invented a method of preserving them for archaeologists to study. He drilled a small hole into the hollow, then poured liquid plaster inside. It set hard, molding itself to the shape of the hollow. Afterward, the surrounding pumice and volcanic ash could be chipped away, leaving a permanent plaster cast. Archaeologists today use a similar technique, but with transparent glass fiber instead of plaster.

◁ *This plaster cast of an adult and child from Pompeii was made using Fiorelli's technique.*

## WHO WAS Guiseppe Fiorelli?

*Born in Naples, Italy, in 1823, archaeologist Giuseppe Fiorelli was Dir Pompeii from 1860 to 1875. He did more than anyone else to investigate and preserve the remains of Pompeii. He developed the important archaeological technique of studying sites layer by layer. This meant that important evidence was left unharmed because archaeologists dug systematically into different levels of the earth. He also set up a training school to teach students how to excavate scientifically. He was widely respected and his skills were recognized around the world. He died in 1896.*

# Food and drink

Roman men and women enjoyed their food, but most ate only one main meal a day. They had a light snack when they got up in the morning, soon after dawn, and another quick bite to eat at noon. Usually they ate bread with a little honey, fruit, or cheese.

Their main meal was *cena* (dinner), eaten after work and school had finished at around three in the afternoon. For wealthy families, who entertained important guests such as business colleagues or visiting politicians, dinner was a formal occasion, with carefully chosen food prepared and served by well-trained slaves. A typical meal might have three courses. First, eggs, snails, or shellfish, served with olives and green herbs. Then the main course: roast meat or poultry, fish cooked in a special sauce, or game, such as wild boar. All these were served with bread, vegetables, and rich sauces. To finish, the Romans ate fresh fruit and nuts.

Cooks seasoned dishes with expensive spices imported from the Far East, or with a strong, salty sauce made from rotten fish. They spent time decorating food, or in trying to make it look like something else, either for fun or to display their skills and their owner's wealth.

## Kitchen basics

This bowl of olives was discovered at Pompeii. Olives were probably eaten with drinks before a meal as they are today. Oil and wine were stored in large pottery jars called *amphorae*. Olive oil was used for cooking many dishes, or as a dip with stale bread. The Romans made olive oil by crushing olives in a press. Olive oil was used for lamp light and bathing as well as for cooking.

## Dinner party

Here, Roman diners from the 2nd century C.E. are enjoying a party. As was usual, they are seated three to a couch. Dinner parties could last for several hours. Guests were entertained between courses by singers, dancers, poets, and musicians. Visual evidence from paintings and mosaics can help people understand how objects found at **excavations** such as Pompeii were used in Roman times.

Ordinary people ate simpler meals, mostly bread with some stewed beans or lentils, onions and garlic, and a little meat, fish, or cheese. Many of the herbs used by modern cooks were used by Roman cooks. Parsley, thyme, fennel, fenugreek, angelica, and mint, plus spices from the East were all used to disguise the taste of bad smelling and bad tasting food. Very poor people survived on "doles," small amounts of grain handed out by the Roman government, or by begging from richer families.

## Cooking stove

This kitchen is in a house in Pompeii. Slaves lit a fire of wood in the space under the stove, and foods were stewed or barbecued. Cooks used saucepans made of bronze, which could be poisonous if not coated inside with copper or silver. Cheaper cooking pots were made of pottery. Only the wealthiest homes had stoves or kitchens. Ordinary families bought hot snacks from bars and food stalls in the streets of many towns, or ate simple, cold meals.

DID YOU KNOW? At Roman meals, belching, spitting, and eating so much you were sick were all allowed! **31**

# Clothes and jewelry

Roman clothes were simple—just long lengths of fabric draped around the body held in place with belts and brooches. Clothes needed no sewing, but still took a long time to make. That was because all cloth for tunics, togas, and women's clothes was woven by hand, from hand-spun thread. Usually thread was made from wool, but silk, imported from India, was used for the finest, most expensive robes. Most cloth was made by slaves, to make garments for their owner's family, or sold in shops or markets. It was dyed bright colors, using plant extracts mixed with urine, or a valuable purple dye made from shellfish.

Children wore similar clothes to adults. Young boys wore a gold or leather lucky charm, called a *bulla,* around their neck. They took it off during a special ceremony when they were around sixteen, to show they were adult. Young girls wore white until they were married, at around fourteen Only then could they wear colored clothes.

## EYEWITNESS

"It would be simpler to count the acorns on an oak tree than to describe all the different hairstyles that women wear today."

*Roman poet Horace (65– 8 B.C.E.)*

## Looking good

This is a **mosaic** portrait of a lady from Pompeii. Rich women wore jewelry made of gold and precious stones; poor women could only afford bronze rings and earrings, and glass beads. Decorated brooches held women's clothes together. Roman men often wore rings. Most women had long hair that they arranged in many different styles. Sometimes braids and curls were fashionable; at other times, a smooth, neat bun was considered elegant.

## Tunics and togas

All Roman men wore a loose, knee-length tunic tied with a rope or leather belt around the waist. Tunics were cool and comfortable, and allowed wearers to move freely. Over the top, men wore a thick cloak, with a hood if they lived in the northern **empire,** or a toga, as in this statue. A toga was a wide piece of cloth about twenty feet (six meters) long, draped around the body and over one shoulder. It was usually worn by rich noblemen as a sign of status because it showed that they did not have to do hard work. **Senators'** togas had a broad purple stripe along one edge.

## Women's clothes

This girl is pouring perfume from a jar. She is dressed in a *stola,* a long, full dress belted above the waist, over a floor-length tunic, and she is wearing sandals. Outside, women covered themselves in a large wool shawl called a *palla* (they were not to be seen by other men), and wore ankle-length leather boots. Roman perfumes were made from flowers, spices, and animal scents, mixed with oil or lard, plus salt to preserve them.

DID YOU KNOW? Roman make-up contained poisons such as lead that could be absorbed through the skin. **33**

# ENTERTAINMENT

The Romans' working day began soon after dawn, but ended by around 2 P.M. One day in every eight was a holiday—usually the time when farmers and craftworkers took their goods to market. There were also many religious festival days. This meant that many Romans had plenty of free time to enjoy music, dancing, going to the theater, listening to poetry, telling jokes and stories, playing games such as dice, or going to watch chariot races and **gladiator** fights. In Rome, the main arena for horse racing was the Circus Maximus, which was rebuilt in the 1st century B.C.E. Alterations continued up to C.E. 400. The Circus Maximus was a huge racetrack, with seats for 250,000 spectators. To see gladiators, people flocked to the Colosseum.

△ The Colosseum was the first permanent **amphitheater** in Rome, and the largest. It was built between C.E. 72 and 80 and consisted of a vast oval arena, surrounded by seats for 50,000 spectators.

▷ A gladiator who killed wild animals was called a **bestiarus**.

# WHO IS Giangiacomo Martines?

*Architect Giangiacomo Martines is in charge of a major project to restore the Colosseum. When the project started in 1995, more than 80 percent of the Colosseum was closed to the public. Martines hopes that when it is completed, more than 80 percent will be open. He says, "Keeping an old monument closed to visitors is like locking a vintage car in a museum—it may be nice to look at, but . . . it won't work."*

## The Colosseum

For almost 2,000 years, the Colosseum has been one of the most famous buildings in Rome. Unlike many ancient sites, it was never lost or forgotten, but for years it was neglected, looted, and vandalized. The last gladiator games were held there in C.E. 404, and the last wild beast hunt in C.E. 523. After becoming Christians, Romans no longer wanted to watch the games because they felt the killing was sinful. Roman **emperors** could also no longer afford them.

△ **Excavations** have revealed this maze of cells, cages, and passages under the sand-covered floor of the Colosseum. Wild animals and gladiators were kept here before a fight, and this is where staff had their stores and offices.

## Trained to kill

Gladiators were slaves, criminals, or prisoners of war. They fought each other or wild animals (mostly from Africa) to amuse bloodthirsty spectators. Some gladiators were specially trained at gladiator schools to make the entertainment more exciting. Successful gladiators became as famous as rock stars today and attracted crowds of fans, but most died horribly.

After around 1700, tourists began to admire the Colosseum as a "noble **ruin**." Today it is one of the best-known monuments in the world. In 2000, it had 2.5 million visitors.

### Archaeology Challenge

Millions of people enjoy visiting ancient monuments. But too many visitors can damage historic sites. Over the centuries, tourists have harmed the Colosseum by chipping off bits of stone as souvenirs. Some experts think visitors should be kept away from the most important monuments so that they will be preserved for scholars to study and future generations to admire. Others do not agree.

## At the baths

Most Roman houses did not have a bathroom. Instead, people visited public baths. Public baths were huge buildings built by the **emperor** or other wealthy people. The entrance fee was very low—most could afford it. Women went to the baths in the morning and men bathed in the afternoon or early evening.

Each bath had several different rooms—hot, cold, damp, or dry. Bathers moved from one room to the other. They wanted to get very hot, so the sweat poured off them, loosening the dirt on their skin. Next a slave smeared olive oil over them, and scraped the mixture off with a blunt metal blade called a *strigil*.

### Baths of Caracalla

Built between C.E. 206 and 217, on the orders of Emperor Septimus Severus and his son, Emperor Caracalla, these massive public baths—the biggest in Rome—had room for 1,600 bathers. They were built of red brick covered with marble, and decorated with statues and **mosaics.** Most of the marble was taken away by a Roman noble family in the 1500s to decorate their own palace.

▽ *The curved part of the* strigil *was used by slaves to scrape olive oil and sweat from a bather's skin.*

## Technology Challenge

Roman baths were heated by an invention called a **hypocaust.** This sent hot air under the **bathhouse** floor. It escaped through hollow channels in the walls, and out through chimneys. The air was heated by a furnace outside the bathhouse walls that was kept burning by slaves.

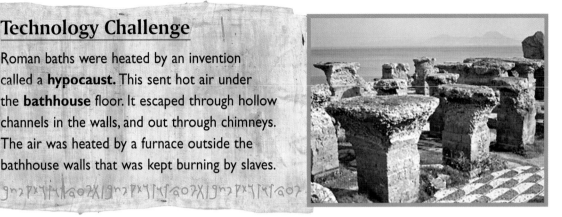

Finally, to feel really clean, bathers jumped into a cool plunge pool. After a bath, women, and some men, rubbed more oil into their skin to soften it. Often, they added a few drops of perfume. Baths were more than just places where you went to keep clean. The Romans went there to meet their friends, to relax, gossip, and exercise. The biggest baths, like the Baths of Caracalla, also had gardens outside, an art gallery, a library, and a snack bar.

### EYEWITNESS

"I live close to the public baths . . . It's dreadful. . . . I hear the strong men doing their exercises. They swing lead weights and grunt and groan. . . . But worse than any of these is the man who likes to sing in the bath, and the bathers who jump in, making a big splash."

Roman writer Seneca (c. 4 B.C.E.– C.E. 65)

## Keeping fit

The Romans believed that exercise was good for them, and there were sports centers close to many Roman baths. Favorite Roman sports included running, throwing the javelin, fencing, swimming, weight-training, and a game similar to volleyball. Throwing the discus, as shown here, was another popular sport.

# TRAVEL, TRANSPORTATION, AND TRADE

U nder Roman rule, the **empire** was peaceful for much of the time. Horse-riders, wagon-drivers, women traveling in cushioned **litters,** and men leading donkeys, pack-horses, or camels all felt safe to make journeys. Officials traveled on government business, farmers traveled to markets, and tourists traveled for fun. Merchants developed networks of long-distance cargo routes, carrying bulky goods by sea.

## Roman ships at Pisa

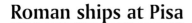

In 1998, workers digging foundations for a new railway station at Pisa, a port in Italy, uncovered the remains of a Roman ship. Since then, fifteen more ships have been discovered, together with the remains of a wooden **wharf, breakwater,** and pier. The ships' cargoes, including many tall pottery jars called *amphorae,* together with their crews' clothes, shoes, fishing tackle, medical supplies, and personal possessions, have also been found.

All these exciting finds are well preserved, even though they have been underwater for about 2,000 years. The site where they were found had once been a harbor, and was still waterlogged. The water and sand helped preserve the ships and their contents, since the air was kept away. Without air, they could not decay or rot.

△ *Archaeologists at work in Pisa, Italy, have found the largest group of ancient vessels ever discovered at one site.*

△ *A **mosaic** from the 3rd century* C.E. *shows the unloading of a cargo ship in the port of Ostia, near Rome. You can see the ship's deep **hull** and two big steering oars.*

Because the site was so wet, the team excavating the Roman ships at Pisa had to use techniques developed by underwater archaeologists—especially for **conserving** ships' timbers. Underwater archaeology is one of the newest areas of archaeological exploration, but it has already provided much important new information about Roman travel and trade.

◁ *Pottery jars, called* amphorae, *were used to carry liquids, such as wine and olive oil. Their long, thin shape made it easy to pack them close together in cargo ships.*

## Archaeology Challenge

The sea contains many hundreds of sunken ships and submerged coastal cities full of exciting evidence for archaeologists, but they are very difficult to find and explore. The first known underwater investigation was in the mid-1400s when a priest hired 1,446 swimmers to look for sunken Roman ships, thought to contain treasure. Since then, divers, miniature submarines, electric currents, sound waves, and underwater cameras have been used to investigate the seabed and look for treasures there.

## WHO WAS Jacques Cousteau?

*Born in France in 1910, Cousteau was an archaeologist, **environmentalist,** photographer, and film-maker. With a colleague he invented a new piece of equipment, called SCUBA (Self-Contained Underwater Breathing Apparatus), to help divers explore the sea. He developed techniques for "digging"underwater (using a huge suction tube) and for raising finds to the surface. His films and television programs introduced the undersea world, and the archaeological evidence hidden there, to millions of viewers. He died in 1997.*

## Crafts and trades

The Roman empire produced a huge variety of goods to sell. France produced wine, wheat grew well in Egypt, olive oil and fine wool came from Spain, Great Britain was famous for tin and furs, honey came from Greece, and slaves came from Germany and many eastern European lands. Roman merchants traded these valuable goods throughout the **empire** and also bought and sold high quality craft goods.

Roman craftworkers trained in workshops by watching older, experienced workers and copying their skills. It took many years of practice to make a handmade piece. Cheaper, **mass-produced** items, such as pottery, were often made by slaves. Shiny red pottery jugs, bowls, and platters from France, known as "Samian ware," were sold all over the empire.

Women were not allowed to train for many trades, but wives often worked alongside their husbands because many shops and craft businesses were based in family homes. Widows, like Eumachia of Pompeii, ran businesses by themselves. Eumachia became so rich she gave money to build a new market hall. Freed slaves also became traders. Some freed female slaves even did jobs normally closed to women, such as doctors or librarians.

▽ *Samian pottery was very popular in the 1st and 2nd centuries. There were Samian ware factories throughout Italy and in Gaul (France).*

### Roman coins

Standard-sized, well-made Roman coins helped trade throughout the empire. Coins were also a reminder of the **emperor's** power. Roman coins were made of gold, silver, and bronze, depending on their value. Gold and silver coins were issued by emperors only; cheaper bronze coins were made on the senate's orders. After 27 B.C.E., all coins were decorated with the emperor's head on one side, and a symbol of Roman power, such as an eagle, on the other. Finding Roman coins help archaeologists date their excavations.

## Trajan's Market, Rome

The Romans invented shopping malls. Trajan's Market, the largest mall, had more than 150 shops on five levels, selling everything from silks and flowers to fresh fish. The market was built around C.E. 107 to celebrate Emperor Trajan's victories. As well as shops, it had a **temple,** libraries, and a law court. It also housed the government offices where poor people lined up to receive regular supplies of grain to feed their families. Here someone is shown buying cloth in the 3rd century C.E.

## Craft skills

This glass jug, drinking cup, and blue dove ornament are from the 1st century C.E. As well as producing beautiful glass pieces like these, the Romans learned to mass-produce objects quickly and cheaply by blowing molten glass into molds. Metalworkers made everyday items, such as cooking pots, from iron, and delicate objects, such as dishes and jewelry, from gold, silver, and bronze.

### EYEWITNESS

"Farm workers, veterinary surgeons, brick-makers, builders and decorators, blacksmiths, bakers, shipwrights, drivers, barbers, metalworkers, water-carriers, polishers, scribes, tailors, teachers, lawyers, bath attendants, gold and silver smiths, dry cleaners, textile workers of all kinds . . ."

Workers in Rome, listed in a government document, C.E. 301

# ROMAN ARCHAEOLOGY TODAY

O ver the centuries, ways of doing Roman archaeology have changed—and so have archaeologists. They are no longer rich treasure-hunters, like the Italian churchman who sent swimmers underwater, or inquisitive artists or energetic landowners with Roman **ruins** on their **estates**. Instead, they can be scientists, historians, divers, gardeners, and people who like dressing up in old clothes. Many work in teams, like the staff of the Leptis Magna **excavations** in Libya, north Africa, so that they can combine their skills.

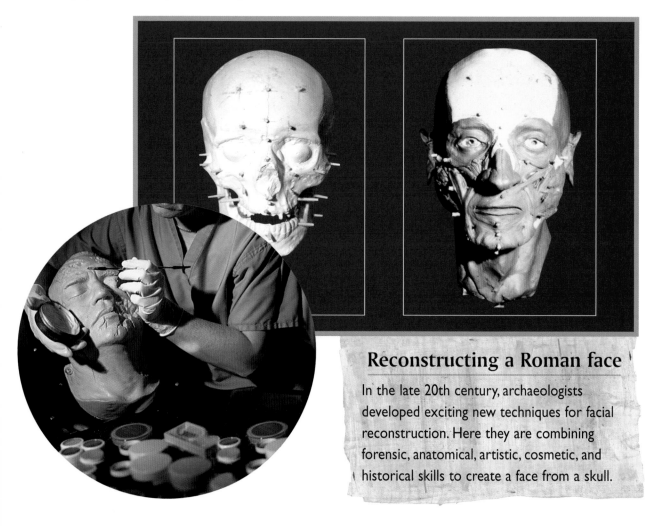

### Reconstructing a Roman face

In the late 20th century, archaeologists developed exciting new techniques for facial reconstruction. Here they are combining forensic, anatomical, artistic, cosmetic, and historical skills to create a face from a skull.

Most archaeologists today are well-trained professionals who work for universities and governments, often on big projects like the excavations at Pisa. Or they join "flying squads," who hurry to save what evidence they can from the past before new building work destroys ancient sites. But some are ordinary people who work as volunteers. And, unlike the early archaeologists, many are women.

Another important difference is that archaeologists no longer publish their findings only for a few, rich, well-educated people to read. Today, they spread the news of their discoveries to a wider audience, through the Internet and on television. Also, they often choose different sites to excavate or **artifacts** to examine. In the past, archaeologists and historians preferred to investigate the lives of famous, powerful people, but today they think it is just as important to find out how ordinary men, women, and children lived.

## Archaeology Challenge

A great deal of Roman evidence has never been "lost." Texts by Roman authors, **inscriptions** carved in stone, and the standing remains of buildings are all clearly there for everyone to see. The challenge faced by many archaeologists today is how to interpret them—that is, how to understand them in the light of new and ever-changing information about Roman times—and how to make them seem interesting and relevant to our lives today.

△ *This reconstruction of a Roman villa in Germany is also a museum. Many historic sites cannot cope with the large numbers of people who want to visit them. So, archaeologists have developed new ways of presenting their findings, for example, by interactive displays in museums, or at heritage centers.*

Roman history is usually divided into two main periods—the **Republic** and the **Empire**. For a time Rome was ruled by the powerful Etruscans from the north of Italy. But in 509 B.C.E. the last Etruscan king of Rome was driven out.

From that time Rome became a republic and a group of officials called **senators** ran the country. Then, in 27 B.C.E., the senate elected the first **emperor**. He was given the title Augustus, which means "person to be respected."

**From 700 B.C.E.**
Many different groups of people lived in Italy at this time, such as the Etruscans and Latins.

**From 600 B.C.E.**
The emergence of the town of Rome, from villages built on seven hills.

### The Roman Republic
### 509 B.C.E. to 27 B.C.E.

**509 B.C.E.**
The last Etruscan king of Rome is overthrown. Roman republic formed.

**264 B.C.E.**
Rome becomes leading town in Italy.

**196 B.C.E.**
The first triumphal arches built in Rome.

**44 B.C.E.**
Julius Caesar is assassinated.

**30 B.C.E.**
Egypt is captured and becomes part of the empire.

**28–19 B.C.E.**
The conquest of Spain is completed.

### The Roman Empire
### 27 B.C.E. to C.E. 476

**27 B.C.E.**
Augustus becomes the first Roman emperor.

**C.E. 43**
Emperor Claudius begins the conquest of Great Britain.

**About C.E. 50**
Roman traders reach Bengal and east India.

**C.E. 75**
Roman traders reach the Sudan in Africa, and set up trade links across the Sahara desert.

**C.E. 79**
Mount Vesuvius destroys Pompeii and Herculaneum.

**C.E. 80**
The Colosseum opens in Rome.

**C.E. 117**
Roman empire reaches its greatest extent under Emperor Trajan.

**C.E. 120s**
Construction of Hadrian's Wall in northern Great Britain begins.

**C.E. 122**
Rome builds frontiers at the edges of the empire (such as Hadrian's Wall in Great Britain).

**About C.E. 200**
Road system is complete throughout the empire.

**C.E. 250s**
Christians are **persecuted** throughout the empire.

**C.E. 284**
Emperor Diocletian divides the Roman empire into a western half and eastern half.

**C.E. 300 to 500**
**Barbarian** invaders enter the Roman empire.

**C.E. 313**
Emperor Constantine accepts Christianity.

**C.E. 324**
Emperor Constantine reunites the two parts of the empire.

**C.E. 330**
City of Constantinople (Istanbul in modern Turkey) founded.

**C.E. 395**
Roman empire divided back into two parts.

**C.E. 410**
Rome is captured by the Visigoths and Great Britain is abandoned by Roman **legions** as they leave to defend Italy from barbarians.

**C.E. 455**
Rome is attacked and destroyed by Vandals.

**C.E. 476**
The last Roman emperor is overthrown. End of the Roman empire in the west.

# TIMELINE OF ROMAN ARCHAEOLOGY

**About 1350–1550**

The Renaissance (re-birth) is a 1800s term for the period in which there was a great revival of interest in the art and learning of ancient Rome and Greece. The Renaissance begins in Italy and spreads throughout Europe.

**1506**

The marble statue of Laocoon and his sons being attacked by serpents is rediscovered and put on display in Rome where it causes a sensation. This famous sculpture has more adventures later, for in 1796 it is taken from Rome to Paris, but returns in 1815 after Napoleon is defeated.

**1763**

Johann Joachim Winckelmann (1717–1768) starts work in Rome. He studies the art collections and the remains of ancient architecture as well as ancient **artifacts**. He also studies the remains of Pompeii and Herculaneum. He writes a highly regarded book *History of Ancient Art* that is based almost entirely on Roman art or Roman copies of Greek originals.

**1800s**

Nathaniel Clayton, owner of Chesters House on Hadrian's Wall, decides to cover over the remains of Chesters Fort with soil as part of his **estate**. On his father's death, John Clayton (1792–1890) decides to start **excavating** the site. Throughout his life he continues to buy land beside Hadrian's Wall and begins excavating the **forts** inside the wall—these include Chesters, Housesteads, Carrawborough Mithraic **Temple**, and Carvoran. After he died, a museum was built on the site to house all the artifacts.

**1860–1865**

Guiseppe Fiorelle is appointed Director of Excavations at Pompeii. Under his direction work becomes more scientific. He develops the important archaeological technique of studying sites layer by layer. He keeps records of exactly where each artifact is found and sets out to **conserve** and preserve the town. He also invents the method of making plaster casts of the body shapes at Pompeii.

**1875**

Rodolfo Lanciani is appointed Director of Excavations in Rome. He is responsible for a number of major discoveries such as the House of the Vestals in the Forum. He becomes an expert in the modern scientific study of **topography**. He compiles a very detailed set of maps of ancient Rome that are still considered the best today. He systematically records vital evidence about ancient Rome during a period when the city is undergoing extensive rebuilding that would otherwise have been lost forever.

**1942**

While plowing some fields near Mildenhall in Suffolk, England, a farmworker spots some metal objects poking up through the ground. He and the owner dig the earth and discover 34 pieces of Roman silver tableware—dishes, goblets, spoons, bowls, and ladles.

**1942–1943**

Jacques Cousteau (1910–1997) made his first underwater films during World War II. He also perfected the aqualung—a piece of breathing equipment that supplies oxygen to divers. Jacques Cousteau also developed techniques for "digging" underwater and raising finds to the surface.

**1960s**

Workmen digging a trench for a new waterpipe in Fishbourne, southern England, accidently discover the remains of a Roman building dating from around C.E. 75. This turns out to be the largest villa discovered in Great Britain so far. Most of its 80 rooms have **mosaic** floors and the villa reflects the luxury of Rome.

**1970s–1990s**

Robin Birley works on the first **excavations** at Vindolanda. This is a 1st century fort near Hadrian's Wall in northern England. In the 1970s, 1980s, and 1990s he finds some remarkable wooden writing tablets in the waterlogged ditches. These tablets reveal what life was like for soldiers and their wives and families on the very edge of the empire.

**1994**

Leptis Magna is one of the best preserved and most important Roman cities in Africa. From 23 B.C.E. it was a major port for sending goods such as oil, grain, and wild animals back to Rome. Since 1994, Dr. Hafed Walda has been leading a team of archaeologists in new excavations on part of Leptis.

**aerial**
photograph, or a view from the air

**altar**
table for offerings and sacrifices outside a temple

**amphitheater**
oval or circular arena surrounded by rows of seats

**ancestral**
belonging to ancestors—the men and women from whom we are descended

**archive**
store or collection of documents

**artifact**
object made by people, such as a tool or an ornament. Archaeologists often use the word "artifacts" to describe the objects they find that were made by people in past times.

**auxiliary**
soldier recruited into the army from conquered peoples in the Roman empire

**barbarian**
name used by Romans for people they thought were uncivilized, and who spoke different languages. Romans thought these languages sounded as if they were saying "baa, baa, baa."

**bathhouse**
building containing baths for communal use

**breakwater**
wall built out into the sea to shelter ships in a harbor by reducing the force of the waves

**campaign**
series of battles and other activities designed to achieve a long-term military aim, for example conquering a particular country

**centurion**
officer in the Roman army who commanded a century of troops

**century**
unit in the Roman army containing about 80 men

**chronicle**
written account of an important event, ordered by the date they occurred

**citizen**
inhabitant of a country who has full civil rights, for example, the right to vote

**civil servant**
government employee

**commemorate**
honor or celebrate the memory of a person or event

**conservator**
archaeologist trained in cleaning, repairing, and preserving objects from the past

**dictator**
person who rules alone with unlimited power, often ignoring other peoples' rights

**emperor**
male ruler of Rome and the Roman Empire. Emperors ruled Rome from 27 B.C.E. until C.E. 476.

**empire**
lands ruled by one strong person or government

**engineer**
person who designs machines, roads, and bridges

**environmentalist**
person who studies or wishes to protect and improve the natural environment

**estate**
large area of land, often including farms, owned by a wealthy family

**excavation**
process of excavating, that is digging up a building or area of land in order to look for ancient objects, ruins, or other evidence of the past

**fort**
building strengthened for military use, often in an important place

**gladiator**
criminal, prisoner, or slave, forced to fight to the death to entertain Roman crowds

**hull**
part of a ship that sits in the water

**hypocaust**
Roman system of heating rooms or water using hot air circulating through underfloor channels

**inscription**
in archaeology, a historical or religious record that is carved, painted, or written on a hard surface such as stone or metal

**legend**
old story that has been handed down from the past

**legion**
unit within the Roman army containing around 5,000 men

**legionary**
soldier recruited from citizens in the Roman empire to serve in a legion

**litter**
portable bed, screened by curtains and carried shoulder-high on long wooden poles

**mass-produced**
made in large numbers, exactly the same, by workers or (in modern times) by machines

**mosaic**
picture or design, usually made from tiny cubes of colored stone

**palynology**
study of ancient pollen to find out what plants existed long ago

**pension**
money paid to a person who has retired from work

**persecute**
be continually cruel to someone, particularly if you do not agree with their beliefs

**philosophy**
study of ideas and ways of thinking

**propaganda**
news or ideas produced in a way to make people believe it is the truth or to damage opposing views

**pumice**
lava from a volcano that has cooled and turned to solid rock

**republic**
country where citizens have the right to elect (choose) the head of state

**reservoir**
place where water is stored, a man-made lake

**ruin**
building or group of buildings that has fallen down or been destroyed

**scholar**
person who studies. Also, someone who has a lot of knowledge.

**senator**
member of the senate—an assembly, or ruling council, of men in Rome who discussed government policies and debated new laws

**slogan**
a short sentence with a message, often political

**survey**
take detailed measurements of a site and examine it for traces of how it was used in the past

**symbolize**
special meaning of a mark or sign. For example, a cross is a symbol of Christianity.

**temple**
large building designed as a home for a god or goddess where people come to worship

**topography**
study of landscape. The position of mountains, rivers, roads, buildings, etc. in a region.

**wharf**
part of a dock where ships unload cargo

# FURTHER READING

Denti, Mario. *Imperial Rome*. Chicago: Raintree, 2001.

Seely, Elizabeth. *Pompeii & Herculaneum*. Chicago: Heinemann Library, 2000.

Sheehan, Sean. *Ancient Rome*. Chicago: Raintree, 2000.

Whittock, Martyn. *The Colosseum & the Roman Forum*. Chicago: Heinemann Library, 2003.

Williams, Brian. *Ancient Roman Homes*. Chicago: Heinemann Library, 2003.

Williams, Brian. *Ancient Roman War and Weapons*. Chicago: Heinemann Library, 2003.